GALGATE IN FOCUS

Ruth Z Roskell

Landy Publishing
2007

ISBN 978-1-872895-75-8

A catalogue record of this book is available from the British Library

Layout by Anita D Forth

Printed by The Naylor Group, Aero Mill, Church, Accrington Tel 01254 234247
Landy Publishing have also published:-

Northward by Anthony Hewitson
Life on the Lancaster Canal by Janet Rigby
The Lancaster Canal in Focus by Janet Rigby
Glimpses of Glasson Dock & Vicinity by Ruth Z Roskell
Bygone Bentham by Joseph Carr
A Century of Bentham by David Johnson
Bentham as it Were by David Johnson
A History of Pilling by Frank Sobee

Some of the above titles are available at a discounted price when ordered direct from the publisher
A full list of the books currently available can be obtained from
Landy Publishing
'Acorns'
3 Staining Rise, Staining, Blackpool FY3 OBU
Tel/Fax 01253 895678 e-mail peggie@peggiedobson.wanadoo.co.uk

INTRODUCTION

Having moved to Galgate from Glasson in the mid-1960's, I have long had an interest in my adopted village and the beautiful surrounding countryside. I moved here when the mill was still operating, the motorway was still being built and the university was a fledgling. I have seen many changes in the village and the immediate vicinity. My children have all enjoyed participating in the children's treat (think of all those paper flowers I have made) and they attended Ellel St John's School.

I embarked on this book following publication of my book *'Glimpses of Glasson Dock & Vicinity,'* although I had been taking and collecting photographs and information on the village for some years. That Galgate is still a village gives me pride and pleasure. One of the things I like best is listening to *'owd Galgaters'* telling of what they remember and what they have been told about the area and its inhabitants. Some of these conversations- they were in the street, on doorsteps, in shops, in pubs, and sometimes on my allotment- are preserved in this book. I hope that the photographs and captions give pleasure. I have enjoyed assembling them and writing about them.

The book would not have been possible without the help of Bill Atkinson of Quernmore, who loaned me his pictures of the village, and Honor Coates (Cornthwaite as was) who loaned me her mother's postcard collection and gave me lots of information. I also thank Sylvia Blanchard,Lilian Corless and Jim Shaw, John and Judith Pye, Paul and Joyce Newsham and Jean Fisher for the use of their pictures. Fred and Sue Downham, Olive Hill,Loraine Greaves and Bill Bradshaw have all been very helpful.

Ruth Z Roskell, nee Lamb
August 2007

Here we see the main road, (called Main Road) that runs through the centre of Galgate. It was originally part of the Preston to Kendal turnpike, built around 1750, when an Act was passed for repairing and widening the road from Preston to Lancaster and then to Heiring Syke between Carnforth and Beetham. The building and maintenance of the roads was the responsibility of companies called *'turnpike trusts,'* which raised funds through the charging of tolls, which varied from 3d for a vehicle drawn by one horse, to 1s for vehicles drawn by four or more horses. There where no tolls taken on stage- coaches. In 1826, the tolls were advertised in the *'Lancaster Gazette,'* when they were to be let for a term of one year. The nearest toll gate was at Scotforth, where, in1825, £460 was taken.

There has been a crossroads in the village for many years, around which the village has developed. The original road turned and carried on along Salford Road, crossing the River Conder by a ford. A bridge was carrying traffic over the river by 1675. The road carried on up Highland Brow into Lancaster.

The wooden slats on the gable end are a form of weatherproofing on the cottage which was known as *'New Cherry Tree Cottage.'* A caped policeman is leaving the cottage probably to patrol round the village on his bike that is propped near the door. Maybe this was PC Thomas who is mentioned later. Certainly he is the man Galgate folk would call *"our bobby."* The upper photograph was taken from the railway bridge called *'Skew Bridge'* because of the angle at which it crosses the road. The photos would have been taken in the early1900s.

MAIN ROAD   GALGATE

4

Here we see a pony and trap, possibly a *'governess cart,'* being driven down the Main Road, with its driver and passengers.

In 1903 it was reported in the *'Lancaster Observer'* that a farmer from Galgate was drunk in charge of a horse and trap. P.C Thomas saw the defendant on the Lancaster road returning from town. Charging along at around 14 miles an hour, he was seen to be leaning out of the trap and was in danger of falling out. The policeman called for him to stop three times. When he eventually reined in the horse, he was found to be drunk, became abusive and used foul language. He was fined 20s with the costs or 14 days in prison, in default. He had another encounter with the police a few weeks later, when he was stopped for the same offence at Scotforth. This time he had a passenger, his wife. Mr Parker, corn & flour dealer, and James Thompson who ran the Co-op at Galgate vouched for his good behaviour and he was *"let off."*

Richard Aldren, who drove a van and two horses for Messrs Birket, was fined 20s after being charged with being drunk in charge of the horses and van. He had been caught by P.C Thomas in Galgate village without lights and had crashed into a telegraph pole. He was found sat at the front of the van trying to urge the horses on.

This is a view taken from the railway bridge and sold as a postcard. In the distance can be seen the chimney and buildings of Galgate silk mill.

The village from Skew Bridge looking North. A travelling fair has set up in Laund's Field. There are two caravans; one is behind the stone building and would have been used for living in, as it has a chimney. The other is a *'Ledge Type'* with extra wide ledges and would have been what the travelling folk would have called a *'packing wagon,'* used to move all the fair ground equipment around the country. It is unusual as it has a mollicroft roof, which where usually used as living vardos. There is also a water barrel on wheels to make it easier for carrying water around the site. The fair ground folk are busy working on a wooden sign which is on the wooden *'work horses.'*

In 1845 the annual sports day attracted many competitors; some came on the newly- opened Lancaster to Preston Railway, arriving at the nearby station. The mills ceased working at 3 pm, allowing the workers to enjoy the day. The sovereign was won by *'Long Dick'* from Preston, who was 6ft 1in and raced barefoot. There were also wrestling matches; many of the participants became spectators after seeing that 17 stone Boardley and 6ft Miller would have the best match of the day.

The finale of the day was the *'gingling match,'* when Sam Battersby from Skerton was bellman. The game consisted of six young men being blindfolded, many obstacles placed around the ground, they then had to try and catch the bellman who was *"finally caught by Nicholson amidst much merrymaking and cheering."*

In 1852 there was also horseracing, with the events taking place over two days, and dances held in the public houses in the evening.

Looking North, about 1900 through the *'Square'* with the *'Crescent'* in the background. The building on the right, with the ornate door surround, at one time was called *'Derwent House'*. It has a sign above the door that informs villagers and passers by that the building houses a *'Public Telephone Call Office.'* It was operated by William James Jolleys, who also was the proprietor of the joinery and wheelwright business.

The three -storey houses on the left were known as the *'Co-operative Houses.'* Most of the buildings would have been constructed in the mid to late nineteenth century, to accommodate the workers arriving to work in the mills.

At this time, some of the businesses in the village were: Mrs Elizabeth Cornthwaite, grocer, draper and general dealer; James Fearing, agent for the Prudential Assurance and Chas Lucas, fried fish and potato merchant. Mrs Clarkson was the midwife and Miss Sharpe was district nurse.

In 1899 the District Nursing Association was established in the village. At the 1906 annual meeting held in February of that year, it was noted that the nurse had attended 11,152 cases and paid 21,399 visits during its existence. Nurse Boden attended 192 cases and paid 3,908 visits the previous year. In that year a *'maternity nurse'* was established in the village. She would charge either 5s or 10s according to the means of the patient. Friends had subscribed £4.10s towards the cost of a bicycle for the maternity nurse. Perhaps she bought it from Richard Burgess' shop.

Looking south towards *'Skew Bridge.'* The white building with the three upper- storey windows was used by Fred Faulkner, the undertaker, who had once worked as the mill joiner. This photograph was perhaps taken on the same day by the man who took the photographs from the railway bridge seen on the earlier pages.

The Crescent with the houses fronting onto *'the new road'* which was opened in early March 1824, when Dolphinholme Band led the procession with flags flying from Burrow Beck to Galgate. The new road was built to avoid the steep hill of *'Galgate Brow.* The passenger coach travelling from Liverpool to Lancaster overturned near the village, with several of the occupants being injured in July 1818. The driver of a passenger coach in 1821 was fined £5 and sent to the House of Correction for one month, for racing a rival coach. The horse and cart was used to move goods from the railway or canal wharfe to the mill. William Parkinson worked as the mill carter making several trips a day.

In the upper picture the white buildings on the right were part of the *'Back of Dragon House.'* They were very small cottages. In 1910 they were occupied by nine families, but were later demolished as *'prone to flooding.'* They could also have been known as *'Fisherman's Row.'* During the floods of 1906 it was reported in the local newspaper *'The Conder reached it's height about 3 o clock and being fed by Whitley Beck, overflowed its banks. Basements of several houses were flooded;*

Fisherman's Terrace behind the Green Dragon got the lion's share of the flood, their gardens under two foot of water and folk had to remain in their bedrooms and wait till the floodwater subsided.'

In the upper picture we are looking towards the South. The milkman's cart and *'milk kits'* can be seen in the middle distance. Perhaps it is John Cornthwaite delivering the milk. The New Inn in the far distance is on the left of the picture. In the lower picture, we see the view North.

The *'Crescent,'* was built in the 1850s, by John Armstong for his workers at the *'New Brick Mill.'* These houses were known as *'Brick Row.'* They had a living room, kitchen, scullery and four bedrooms and outside they had small gardens, yards and *'appurtenances.'* After his death in 1858 they were auctioned and described as *'twenty four cottages with sculleries known as Galgate Crescent.'* The shop with the sign above the door was run by Miss Hannah Stringfellow, a *'provision dealer.'* She was the niece of George and Mary Swarbrick, who had run the shop in the early 1890s

It could be a Monday as they have hung the washing out to dry over the railings.

In 1896 there was a serious accident when Joseph Williamson, who lived at no 21, was getting ready for bed and was turning down the oil lamp when it exploded and set fire to his clothing. A police sergeant and constable with Mr T Cornthwaite, who were all trained ambulance men, came to his aid.

The cattleman could be Dick Braithwaite in the early years of the century.

The Police Station seen on the right, a fine stone building, was built in 1897 and had two cells. Galgate has not been without crime over the years evidenced by a report in the *'Lancaster Gazette'* in November 1804. *'Stolen off Widow Turner of Galgate, two bedgowns, two shifts, a pair of shoes, a pair of patterns, caps, ribbons and various other articles, by a young women about 17 or 18 years of age, called*

herself Alice Ogden wore a black bonnet, shabby petticoat without stays, dark complexion and full in the breasts.' There are no records to tell if she was ever apprehended, but if she had been, she would have been imprisoned in Lancaster Castle and if found guilty could have been transported to Australia or sentenced to death by hanging

Here we are looking up *'Stoney Lane,'* which is one of the older lanes in the village; it is thought to be part of the Roman road from Ribchester to Lancaster. The trees of Ashley Farm can be seen. In 1912 John Littledale Parker who described himself as *'the patentee of the motor sprung wheel'* lived there. The walls in front of them enclose Whitley Beck, which runs under the *'New Inn'* and Main Road before joining the River Conder.

In the 1890's Thomas Shuttleworth was the *'beer-house and cow keeper'.* The *'Mason's Arms,'* was put up for auction in 1897 and was described; as *'an old established and well known Beer House. Situated in the village of Galgate, fronting the Turnpike Road with garden, brew house and appurtences.'* Lot 2 was described as *'all those two fields situated in Galgate and known as the 'Lawnd Fields' containing 5acres 3rood and 26 perch or thereabouts, is near the Turnpike Road and the Railway Station.'* The two lots were in the occupation of Thomas Shuttleworth.

James Cottam Taylor was licensee of the *'Mason's Arms'* in 1908 when this photo was taken. Two years later a fire broke out among hay that was being stored in one of the outbuildings belonging to the pub. Galgate Fire Brigade was sent for but could not save the roof from falling in. The final tenant was Mrs Margaret Taylor, a widow with four children who was refused a new licence in 1911. The year before in January, 1910 Thomas Fox was charged with being drunk in the pub. He was found asleep in the corner by the fire, and was fined 10s. *'The Lancaster Guardian'* headed the article *'Fox Asleep at Galgate.'*

Here we see Jim and Mary Shaw outside Mitchell's *'New Inn'* probably around the late 1920s or early 30s. Earlier beer-house keepers there have been: Thomas Braithwaite, who also kept a few cows in the stalls at the side of the building. He would walk them down to Launds Fields and also take them down to the Conder Bridge, for them to drink. In the 1860s Nathaniel Thornton was the innkeeper; his neighbour Richard Pope was a tea dealer. In 1863 whilst he was away from home, a fire broke out at the shop and cottage, the building was saved with only the loss of some books and furniture.

In 1870 William Helme was at the *'New Inn'*. Before that he had been running the *'Bridge Inn'*. Some of the other inns and beer-houses in the village were: *'The Whittle & Steel'*, *'The Plough'*, *'The Cross Keys'*, *'The Bull & Butcher'*, *'The Mason's Arms'* and *'The Shovel & Broom'* which was down a ginnel on Salford Road.

Next door to the *'New Inn'* was Mrs Cornthwaite's grocery shop. Her two daughters Belle and Katie qualified as teachers in 1906 and went on to teach at Thurnham School, which was closed in 1953.

Here we see the Burgess Cycle shop situated in the right of the building in the Square. The arrow pointing into the square is attached to the side of the building on Chapel Street, with the ivy covered building of the *'Green Dragon'* in the background. The business was started by Richard in the early 1900s. He had been born in Yorkshire around 1864, crossed the Pennines for work, found employment at the mill as a silk card winder and lived on Chapel Street with his relation John Fawcett and his family. He married Mary Ann West around 1887. They had fifteen children and Mary also found time to run a grocery and provision shop next to the cycle shop. Their children established many businesses in the village.

Young Richard Burgess was born around 1894. He could be one of these young lads outside his father's shop. When he was a young lad, he would go on his bike twice a week to Dr. Dean's surgery to pick up the medicine for the folk of the village. He later moved round the corner onto the Crescent where he had a shop next to *'Mainstone House.'* The advert is from 1960 and was in a booklet of rambles around the area.

The garage was named after land in the area called *'Launds Field.'*

Another view taken in the early 1900s of the square, showing both shops belonging to the Burgess family, perhaps it is one of the younger members of the family outside the grocery shop in the perambulator/ bassinette. Richard Burgess, with Bill Kitchen started a bus service from Galgate to Dalton Square in Lancaster, towards the end of 1920. Richard held Galgate's first Hackney Carriage Licence and Public Service Vehicle Licence to run a motor omnibus. Their first bus was a Ford Tonner Model T: they then acquired an old London omnibus, which had had the top removed. There was no windscreen; it had solid tyres with a 7ft 6in wheelbase. They would drive it up to Abbeystead and to Garstang. Teddy Pennington would go with them after they had lifted him onto the passenger seat as he suffered from dwarfism and made his living by selling peanuts which he carried around the district in a basket.

In May 1922 Richard was involved in a accident between the Infant School and Ward Field Farm. Richard with his conductor John Pedder had left the *'Green Dragon'* at 12.45 pm and was on his way to Lancaster in his red bus, when John Storey, who ran the green Garstang bus left the *Green Dragon* at 12.50 pm, caught up with him and tried to overtake him when a car appeared coming from Lancaster. John didn't fall behind, but kept alongside and ran into Richard's bus, which resulted in the wooden mudguard being smashed. P.C Stibbons came along to sort out the *'boy racers'* and after John appeared in court he was fined £5 with £3.3s advocate's fees.

Central Garage on Main Road was first run by R.L.R Alston in the early 1930s. He advertised that he specialised in *'lights, radiators, magnetos, bells, radios and accessories.'*

Bill Kitchen took over the garage in the mid 30s. Over the years the garage expanded and in 1955 Bill's daughter Jean, who had married Dick Fisher took over the running. As well as selling petrol, they began selling cars. The line of cars in the photo is from when they first started selling Minis about 1960. The garage is now run by their daughter Janet with her husband Brian.

During the war John and Bill Kitchen started to manufacture aeroplane parts in the workshop next to the garage. An air raid shelter was situated next to the workshop. After the war, the workshop was changed to an engineering and car part workshop. They employed around fifteen people from the village in the 1950s when Albert Atkinson was foreman.

Bill Kitchen was a Galgate lad. His mother was Margaret Burgess, from the cycle shop in the Square and she had married William 'Pop' Kitchen, the village butcher. With his brother John and uncles Fred and Frank Burgess they became interested in motor cycles and started riding on the sands and grass tracks in the area, Bill eventually became the country's first grass track champion. In the 1930s he started to ride for 'Belle Vue Aces' and also raced at the T.T. Races with his friend Lionel Cordingley, who had married a local lass, Ethel Tyson. Bill would represent his country on numerous occasions and was captain of the team in 1939.

The 'Belle Vue Aces' with Pop Kitchen on the far left in the overcoat and Dick Fisher next to him. Dick had been mentored by Bill in his early years, and qualified for his first world championship in 1956.

Here we see Grandad Kitchen in his butcher's coat, with Billy Jenkinson, Miles Fishwick, Bill Kitchen, Eric Kitchen, Wilf Cornthwaite, Albert Waddington, Bill Eastwood, Frank Illingworth, Dick Burgess in the bowler hat, Tommy and Jessie Hall, Jack Kitchen and Tommy Peck on the bike.

'Salford' means 'ford by the willow trees.' Salford Row was part of the original road which forded the River Conder on the way into Lancaster. It went through the Six Arches Bridge which spans the river and the road. On Joseph Locke's survey for the line of the railway in 1836, the plan was for it to run on the land between the *'Whittle and Steel'* and the cottages, but it was later changed to run at the other side of the pub.

The viaduct's first stone was laid on the 28th June 1838, the day of Queen Victoria's coronation. Several medals were deposited under it, amidst great celebrations, with up to five hundred people parading around the village. They were led by the *'Galgate Band of Music'* before sitting down to a meal at the Silk Mill with many of the *'navigators'* taking part in the celebrations. During construction, a stage was built 40 foot above the road, to facilitate the travelling crane which was used to raise the stones.

The little girl in the road has been well wrapped up in a plaid shawl. The cottages on Salford Road would have been constructed at different times, the ones nearest the pub probably being built first. At one time these three housed more than one family as they are over three storeys with access from the back. In the 1870s Nancy Allen lived at No 1 Back of Salford Row, with house owner Elizabeth Butler living at No 1 Salford Row.

When work was done in one of them, a little window was discovered in the attic, revealing that the plasterer had used hair from a chestnut and a grey horse in the plaster.

The cottage with the sign over the door next to the ginnel was the home and shop of shoe maker Robert Gillet; who lived there for over forty years from the early 1850s.

Two views of Ellel House, situated next to the silk mill. It was built before 1792. It was the home of the mill owners and managers. From the 1860s to the 1880s it was the home of James Robinson, the Managing Director. In the 1890s it was the home of George and Emily Satterthwaite with their daughter, Mabel Grace, whose governess was Henrietta Menges. The cook and maidservant lived in; the housekeeper lived next door .One of the mill ponds next to the house was used as an ornamental pond, full of water lilies. The water never froze over as it was heated with water from the mill.

The boys and girls, thirty of them, outside the Infant School in the early 1900s. In 1909 the infant school was closed when seventy children caught measles.

The Infant School was situated in the village on Main Road, next to the Police Station and was built around 1860.

The first school in the area was up Stoney Lane, and was based in a small cottage, once known as *'The Doll's House.'* The last schoolmaster was George Blezard, who lived there in the 1840s. Elizabeth Gardner was the school mistress.

During September 1845 the *'New British School'* was opened, on Stoney Lane. John Armstrong, the silk mill owner, paid for a school to be built in the village. It was originally to be a one- storey building for 150-200 children, but another storey was added to accommodate a lecture room capable of holding 300-400 people, for the use of the societies that then met in the village pubs and beerhouses, so they could use it and not come into contact with intoxicating liquers. When it was opened a tea party was held and speeches given by John Armstrong and Mr Edward Dawson who said already seventy *'night scholars'* had enrolled. The building is now the Catholic Church.

The Junior School, or, as it was locally known, *'the Top School,'* was built around 1860 near the chapel on Chapel Lane, named after the chapel that has been in Ellel since 1154. The post box in the wall is Victorian and probably one of the last in the area.

The school was originally the *'National School'*. It closed in 1967 when Ellel St John's School opened on Chapel Street at a cost of £29,000, bringing together infants and juniors for the first time.

The boys and girls had separate play grounds and entrances to keep them apart. These junior girls, with Nora Parkinson on the front row kneeling, would have been taken around 1920.

The children who were Roman Catholic had to go to Thurnham School, a journey of over two miles, walking through the fields come rain or shine.

Major celebrations were held in the village in 1887 to celebrate Queen Victoria's Golden Jubilee and in 1889 when the first *'Children's Treat'* was held, 300 children took part in the procession which was led by the Galgate Drum and Fife Band.

These photographs are from later years, perhaps as late as 1920 judging by the presence of a *'soldier'* on Britannia's cart. On the other photograph William Parkinson with his pony *'Wild Wave'* at the beginning of a jolly day.

The Galgate F.C team from 1932/33 with the men in their suits wearing large rosettes. From left to right on the back row are:-W. Shaw, John Ribchester, Tom Crossley, B. Smith, Jack Illingworth, Harry Cornthwaite, Robert Bowker, Jack Bowker and S. Wilson, seated are T. Illingworth, T. Hayhurst, Captain Jim Billsborough, E. Sharples, John Cornthwaite and F. Pye. At one time the team's colours were yellow trimmed with black.

The First team taken in 1947 on the recreation field at Galgate. Some of the team are Eric Quick, Maurice Illingworth, Norman Blundell, Tommy Bowker, Jack Briscow, and Ronnie Singleton.

The Second XI from the same year. The goalkeeper was Alan Eccles and some of the team were Gordon Preston, Harold Parks and Norman Kay.

Here we see *'Station Bottom'* with one *'t'* on the photograph. It was also known as *'Violet Bank'*. In 1921, Agnes Cornthwaithe who lived at Violet Bank had to give evidence in court about a baby that was abandoned on the canal by a young girl from Preston. They had travelled on the train in the same compartment to Galgate. The young girl had come to the village for an interview as a farm servant and had abandoned the child to try and get the job. She was bound over for good behaviour and returned to Fulwood Institute.

The station was built by *'The Lancaster and Preston Junction Railway'* and was first opened on 25th June 1840. Rioting took place between the English and Irish navvies at the end of September 1838, when up to 200 English navvies set off from Hampson Green and caught several Irish navvies at the *'Green Dragon'* from where they chased them into Lancaster and gave them a beating. Two of the ringleaders were sentenced to *'three months hard labour:'* The disturbance had started over the Irish working for lower pay. The station consisted of stationmaster's house and building on the *'down'* side and on the *'up'* side was a waiting shelter. When the station closed to passengers on May 1st 1939, Mr Thompson was the station master. It was briefly reopened on the night of Sunday August. 11. 1940, when Ken *'Snakehips'* Johnson was travelling from London to appear at the Winter Gardens at Morecambe. The train was delayed by several hours because of the fog, so the band were taken off the train at Galgate and bussed to Morecambe.

A BIRDS EYE VIEW FROM RAILWAY GALGATE   Nº 25

The first meeting to discuss a railway between Preston and Lancaster was held in Lancaster in 1836. Joseph Locke made a survey in the same year. By March 1840 the work was *'making capital progress'*. It was also noted in early June that *'Skew Bridge'* had been tried, with a heavily laden train of wagons being taken across the bridge.

The *'Lancaster & Preston Junction Railway'* was opened on the 25th June 1840 with much ceremony. Nine first- class carriages and three second -class carriages were drawn by two engines. The passengers were accompanied by a brass band for their journey which took an hour and twenty minutes, as caution was taken. When it was travelling over the embankment at Galgate there was a slight rolling movement, but it wasn't noticed by the passengers. There was great excitement when the train slowly crossed *'Skew Bridge.'* On the return journey they crossed at a faster speed.

The narrow footpath that ran to the railway station was reached from the little gate that was at the side of Skew Bridge and Launds field. It became disused with the shutting of the station to passengers in 1939, but continued to be used by the rail workers for some time before being finally closed and a wall built to enclose the area.

GALGATE FROM THE RAILWAY   Nº 26

The Lancaster Canal was opened on the 22nd November 1797. The original idea had been broached by merchants from Lancaster and Preston as the only way to move goods was by sea or pack horse. The roads were described by travellers as *"infernal highways scarcely passable and infested with robbers."*

John Rennie surveyed the area for the canal in 1791& 1792 and Archibold Millar was appointed as resident engineer. Work on the canal around Galgate ran from 1793 to 1797 when the *'cutters'* or *'navvies'* came from all over the country to work. When the aqueduct was being built over the River Conder, Millar visited the site and found that Pinkerton and Murrey were using inferior soft stone, a different stone to what Rennie had specified. Stone would have been brought down from Ellel Quarry and one from the other side of Ellel Grange by horse and cart for the building project.

A convoy of boats carrying local dignitaries and members of the *'Leeds and Liverpool Canal'* committee accompanied a boat containing limestone which had been brought from north of Carnforth the night before to Galgate, where the *'Ant'* had brought a load of coal and cannel from Preston the previous evening. With much ceremony the cargoes where exchanged.

This aerial view shows *'Pear Tree Farm,'* where the women who lived and worked on barges would come to pick up fresh milk or eggs. Just over the canal bridge, hidden in the trees is the mortuary that was used for any deaths on the canal.

Special trains travelled from Bolton to bring anglers to fish at Galgate. In 1904 there were 940 fisherman spread around the canal, by 1910 there were over a thousand arriving to fish and they stretched from *'Broken Back Bridge'* to the southern end of Bay Horse.

The *'Double Bridge'* is unique on the Lancaster Canal. It is an access bridge and it was built to accommodate two land owners who would not share the same bridge, so a substantial wall runs between it to keep the two tracks separate. One of the many public footpaths in the area crosses the bridge.

The Glasson junction or *'turnover'* bridge was built between 1823 and 1825 of sandstone ashlar. It was constructed so that the barges could be taken onto the Glasson branch without the horses being unharnessed. If they were staying on the main canal, the horses would be led over the bridge. The lock keeper's cottage is close to this bridge and is known as *'Lodge Hill Cottage.'*

ELLEL HALL

Ellel Hall was built around 1700 on the site of an earlier building. In 1688 *'William Rippon of Hareappletree and Ellel Hall'* was mentioned in a petition. *'William Charnock of Ellel Hall'* was mentioned in a will in 1708. By the 1720s, Thomas Jackson was living at the hall. Not much is known of the owners until Abraham Rawlinson died at the hall in 1803. His horses, carriages and coach as well as two brass field pieces plus several pistols and firearms were advertised for sale in the local paper by his nephew, John Ford, who lived at the hall for a short time. In the early 1820s William Hinde, who owned the mill at Dolphinholme, resided there. Then it came back into the Ford family when Abraham Rawlinson Ford, who had been born at the hall in 1813, succeeded to the property when he *'came of age'* in 1834. He lived there till his death in 1849, when it passed to his only surviving brother, William. After his death, the estate was bought by Lord Ashton in 1898.

The hall and estate had around 500 acres of land. There was a large landscaped garden with two *'monkey puzzle'* trees. A *'cork oak'* and *'holm oak'* are still in situ near the hall, in the garden that was separated from the house when a the new road was laid through the grounds in the early 1800s. *'The kiln field'* next to the canal, with its limekiln, was used to produce quick lime for use on the land, or lime whitewash, which was believed to act as a disinfectant on the inside and outside of buildings. The hall owned the wharf at the canal bridge. When the hall was auctioned in 1898 there was a coachman's house and gardener's lodge as well as piggeries, greenhouse, vineries and a peach house. Archery grounds had been built. Mr Eric Dunnet lived at the hall from the 1950s till his death in the 1990s. During that time he had various business ventures, one of which was the hens he kept in large battery huts near the wall.

ELLEL GRANGE

Ellel Grange was commissioned to be built in 1857 by William Preston, a Liverpool merchant who had been born at Pilling. The Grange was finished in 1860. The architect was William Weightman of Liverpool. Mr Preston had bought the estate in 1856, demolished the old hall and had the Italianate villa with pseudo campanile tower, inspired by Osborne House, Queen Victoria's home on the Isle of Wight, built. Some furnishings for the interior were made by Gillows of Lancaster. The large building contained many rooms including a ladies' entrance and bachelor's wing.

It was built close to where the original house had stood. William did not live very long after completion. He was made High Sheriff of Lancashire in 1865, but by 1871 his widow Margaret was living with her daughter of the same name at the house, looked after by many servants including nurse Mary Hazlehurst. Their son George inherited the estate. After his death in 1891, his only daughter Margaret Helena inherited the estate. In 1907 she married Thomas Giles Sandeman who had been born in Portugal and she died in1945. The estate later passed to N.G Sandeman and was auctioned in 1979. It now houses Ellel Ministries.

A winter view of Knowe Hill Farm in Ellel:

The farm was advertised to be let November 1823 as *'a good dwelling house with barn and suitable outbuildings and 23 acres of arable meadow and pasture, being tithe free.'* The tenant was Leonard Ewen. In 1902 Thomas Foxcroft; an army pensioner, had his case dismissed after being caught trespassing in pursuit of game at the farm, when it was occupied by Richard Corless.

Things haven't always run smoothly between the farmers in Ellel as can be seen from a case from January 1870, when Thomas Ellwood brought an action against John Drinkall for the damage caused to crops when his stock strayed onto the other's land. John was fined £1 10s for the damage his bull did to Thomas' cow!

A winter's day picture taken of Kit Brow Farm in Ellel. When James Jolly lived at the farm he had a sale in February 1871, when some of the machinery, livestock and produce were auctioned. In 1922, Mr Rhodes from the farm suffered a broken leg, when he was attacked by a *'tup,'* which is a male sheep. Another farm worker to be injured in 1909 was John Heaton. He was hedging at Scale House Farm when he nearly severed his leg at the ankle. This was unfortunate as his other leg was made of cork as he'd lost it some years previously in an accident with a circular saw.

Ellel Moor was *'inclosed'* by a special *'Act for inclosing diverse, parcels, waste grounds or common in Ellel'* in1756, and laid out into farms brought into cultivation by having the land cleared of rushes, whins or gorse, alder bushes and heather. It was then drained and trenched before it could be worked on.

'St Mary's Hospital for Infectious Diseases' was opened in April 1889. It contained accommodation for twelve patients, and was for the use of any residents living within one mile from the centre of the village. It was situated just out of the village at Smith Green on the road to Dolphinholme. The interior furnishings had been provided by Mr & Mrs Preston from Ellel Grange. Dr. Parker was appointed visiting medical man at a salary of £10 per year or the patients could employ their own doctor. The funds needed to run the hospital were raised by public subscriptions, donations & concerts. The first concert to raise funds had been held the week previously and was very well attended with people packing the large schoolroom. It resulted in £5 15s 9d being raised. It was supposedly never used for the purpose and instead used as a dwelling.

The site was purchased by Pennine Bee Farm in 1948/49. The picture was taken by one of the family in 1952. The flag is flying, because George VI passed on his way to a shooting party at Abbeystead, the year before his death. The building continued to be used up until the early 1960s when it was demolished.

In 1809 an estate at Smith Green was advertised to be let in 'The Lancaster Gazette' and consisted of 'dwelling house, with suitable outbuildings and several closes of land, containing 39 acres, occupied by Henry Threlfall.' In the centre of the estate there was a dry marl pit, the contents of the pit being clay containing lime, which would have been used on the fields as a fertiliser and also a cottage and smithy which could have been the reason for the area's name.

There were several quarries in the Ellel area. The main one was *'Ellel Cragg Quarry.'* The stone was fine sandstone or grit-stone, a much finer stone than found in the quarries in Lancaster, so was used for building some of Lancaster's finest building. The Custom House on the quay was built from stone from Ellel and the pillars at the front of the building were cut from one piece of stone. In 1849 Thomas Murgatroyd sold stone to the value of £47 13s 10d from Ellel Quarry to Mr Rothwell of Foxholes for his building projects. Some of the stone was described as *'long stone, rubble, front stones and cube stones.'* In 1875 they advertised in *'The Lancaster Guardian'* for *'wallers and quarrymen.'* They were looking for six good quarrymen to work for 30s a week. Earlier in July 1872 Messrs. Amos & Jas Murgatroyd, builders from Cockerham put an advert in *'The Lancaster Guardian'* telling masons and builders that they had reopened *'Mainstones Quarry'* at Yeat House, Ellel and they were prepared to supply builders with local stone at reasonable prices. When Thomas died in 1870 his widow Elizabeth married Thomas' cousin, James. They continued to live at Cockerham and operate the quarry. The stone from these quarries was sandstone and would have been used for local building purposes. J.A Jackson Ltd of Preston was the last firm to operate the quarry, when stone was taken and used for the building of the Blackpool motorway (M55) in the 1970s.

Here we see the memorial stone on Green Lane. The stone was raised in memory of Elizabeth Nelson who died aged 31 years defending her honour on the night of 11th January 1866. She had left her employer Mr Millar's home at Skerton to take a letter to his farm at Burrow. The next morning the weather was very cold and when Thomas Wilkinson was driving his horse and cart down the narrow, little used, Green Lane, he found her body lying covered in snow, with no signs of footprints anywhere. He went to tell P.C.Harrison at Galgate. Two local men were arrested. One, John Cottam, was charged but not put on trial, perhaps because the blood on his trousers may have come from his job as a horse breaker. Forensic medicine had yet to make the advances to clear up such matters. Suspicion also fell onto PC Harrison through his having moved the body and having it washed before a fuller examination. There had been a similar incident, thankfully not resulting in death, on nearby Chapel Lane three months previously, and the victim described her attacker as *'a little man in dark clothing wearing a wide-awake hat'*. John Cottam died in 1889 at Halton when he was dragged to death whilst breaking in a horse.